D1716180

First Look at Languages

My First Look
at Spanish

by Jenna Lee Gleisner

cat
gato
(GAH-toh)

dog
perro
(PEH-rroh)

Bullfrog
Books

Ideas for Parents and Teachers

Bullfrog Books let children practice reading informational text at the earliest reading levels. Repetition, familiar words, and photo labels support early readers.

Before Reading

- Discuss the cover photo. What does it tell them?

- Read through the introduction on page 4 and book guide on page 5.

Read the Book

- "Walk" through the book and look at the photos. Let the child ask questions. Point out the photo labels. Sound out the words together.

- Read the book to the child, or have him or her read independently.

After Reading

- Prompt the child to think more. Ask: Have you heard or spoken Spanish before? Practice saying the Spanish words in this book.

Bullfrog Books are published by Jump!
5357 Penn Avenue South
Minneapolis, MN 55419
www.jumplibrary.com

Library of Congress Cataloging-in-Publication Data

Names: Gleisner, Jenna Lee, author.
Title: My first look at Spanish / by Jenna Lee Gleisner.
Description: Minneapolis, MN: Jump!, Inc., 2020.
Series: First look at languages | Includes index.
Audience: Ages: 5–8 | Audience: Grades: K–1
Identifiers: LCCN 2019031151 (print)
LCCN 2019031152 (ebook)
ISBN 9781645273097 (hardcover)
ISBN 9781645273103 (ebook)
Subjects: LCSH: Spanish language—Textbooks for foreign speakers—English—Juvenile literature.
Classification: LCC PC4129.E5 G56 2020 (print) | LCC PC4129.E5 (ebook) | DDC 468.2/421—dc23
LC record available at https://lccn.loc.gov/2019031151
LC ebook record available at https://lccn.loc.gov/2019031152

Editor: Jenna Trnka
Designer: Michelle Sonnek
Translator: Annette Granat

Photo Credits: irin-k/Shutterstock, cover (top left); RemarkEliza/Shutterstock, cover (bottom left); sylv1rob1/Shutterstock, cover (right); cynoclub/Shutterstock, 1; Rawpixel.com/Shutterstock, 3; AnujinM/Shutterstock, 5; Rob Marmion/Shutterstock, 6, 17; nadianb/Shutterstock, 7; Monkey Business Images/Shutterstock, 8–9; karamysh/iStock, 10–11; Paul Brady Photography/Shutterstock, 12–13; Syda Productions/Shutterstock, 14–15; Artazum/Shutterstock, 16–17; wavebreakmedia/Shutterstock, 18–19; FatCamera/iStock, 20–21; Maks Narodenko/Shutterstock, 24.

Printed in the United States of America at Corporate Graphics in North Mankato, Minnesota.

Table of Contents

car
carro
(KAH-roh)

Introduction to Spanish

Where Is Spanish Spoken?

Spanish is spoken in countries around the world, such as Mexico, Puerto Rico, Spain, Cuba, Dominican Republic, and many countries in Central and South America.

How It Differs from English

- The Spanish language uses the same alphabet as English. But it has an additional letter. It is the ñ (the "ny" sound). The symbol above the ñ is called a tilde.

- There are special sounds for "ll" (the "y" sound) and "rr" (a rolled "r").

- Unlike the English language, the "h" is silent.

Accents

Accent marks in Spanish are written over the vowels á, é, í, ó, and ú. They tell the reader which syllable should be emphasized.

You can speak Spanish, too! Let's learn!

Book Guide

This book follows Alma during a typical day. She speaks Spanish. We will learn what her family members, teachers, and friends are called in Spanish. We will also learn the Spanish words for common items we see and use every day.

There are three labels for each word. The first is the English word. The second is the Spanish word. The third is how we pronounce, or say, it. The stressed syllable is in uppercase.

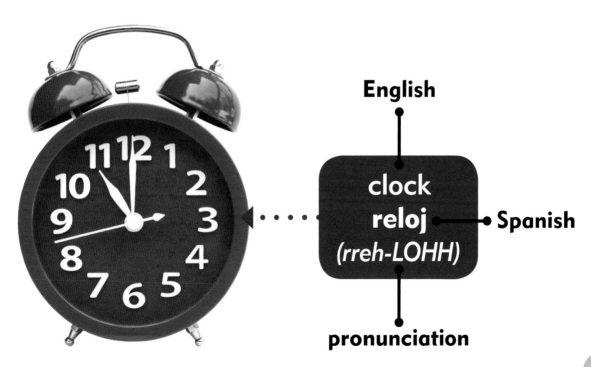

English

clock
reloj
(rreh-LOHH)

Spanish

pronunciation

Let's Learn Spanish!

This is Alma.

She speaks Spanish.
Let's learn!

Spanish
Español
(ehs-pahn-YOHL)

grandmother
abuela
(ah-BWEH-lah)

father
padre
(PAH-dreh)

brother
hermano
(ehr-MAH-noh)

mother
madre
(MAH-dreh)

sister
hermana
(ehr-MAH-nah)

family
familia
(fah-MEE-lee-ah)

This is her family.

What family members do you live with?

Can you say them in Spanish?

grandfather
abuelo
(ah-BWEH-loh)

This is their kitchen.

Look at the Spanish words.

Some look like English words.

Which ones are they?

Say them!

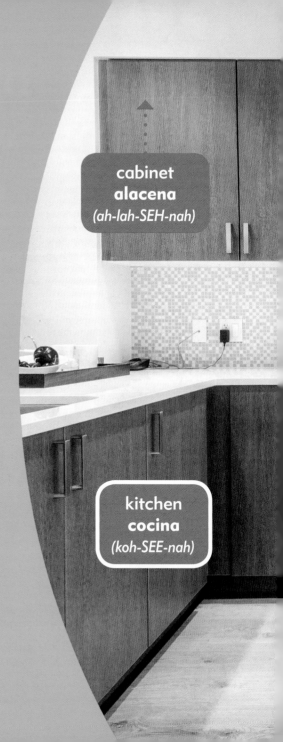

cabinet
alacena
(ah-lah-SEH-nah)

kitchen
cocina
(koh-SEE-nah)

microwave
microondas
(mee-kroh-OHN-dahs)

refrigerator
refrigerador
(rreh-free-heh-rah-DOHR)

oven
horno
(OHR-noh)

floor
piso
(PEE-soh)

napkin
servilleta
(sehr-vee-YEH-tah)

table
mesa
(MEH-sah)

plate
plato
(PLAH-toh)

fork
tenedor
(teh-neh-DOHR)

knife
cuchillo
(koo-CHEE-yoh)

spoon
cuchara
(koo-CHAH-rah)

Alma sets the table for breakfast.

This is Alma's bedroom.

See the Spanish word for bed.

Can you sound it out?

bedroom
dormitorio
(dohr-mee-TOH-ree-oh)

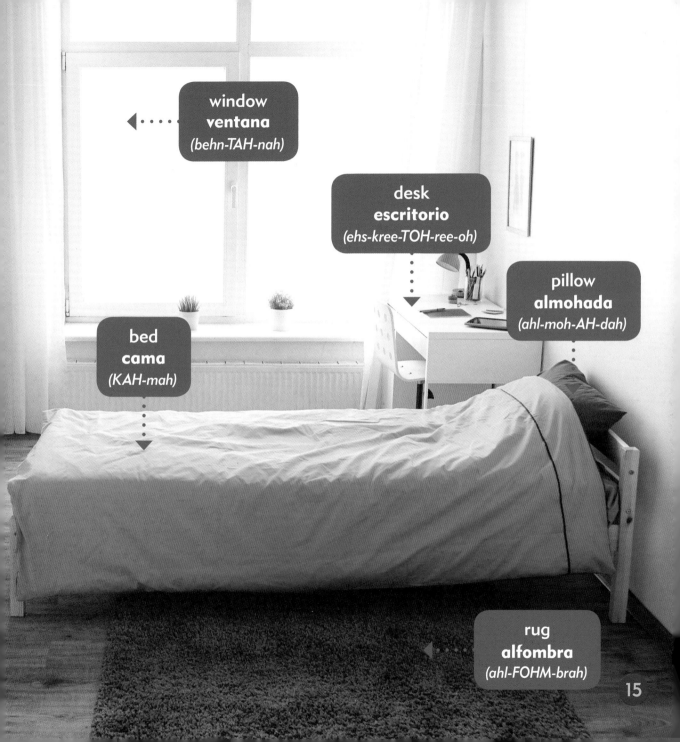

window
ventana
(behn-TAH-nah)

desk
escritorio
(ehs-kree-TOH-ree-oh)

pillow
almohada
(ahl-moh-AH-dah)

bed
cama
(KAH-mah)

rug
alfombra
(ahl-FOHM-brah)

15

mirror
espejo
(ehs-PEH-hoh)

bathroom
baño
(BAH-nyoh)

shower
ducha
(DOO-chah)

sink
lavamanos
(lah-vah-MAH-nohs)

toilet
inodoro
(ee-noh-DOH-roh)

16

Alma gets ready for school.

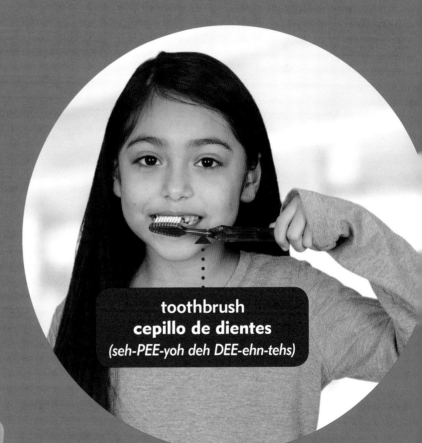

toothbrush
cepillo de dientes
(seh-PEE-yoh deh DEE-ehn-tehs)

This is her classroom.

Her teacher helps.

classroom
salón de clases
(sah-LOHN deh KLAH-sehs)

18

teacher
maestra
(mah-EHS-trah)

student
alumna
(ah-LOOM-nah)

book
libro
(LEE-broh)

paper
papel
(pah-PEHL)

pencil
lápiz
(LAH-pees)

19

outside
afuera
(ah-FWEH-rah)

trees
árboles
(AHR-bohl-ehs)

friend
amigo
(ah-MEE-goh)

ball
pelota
(peh-LOH-tah)

grass
césped
(SEHS-pehd)

sky
cielo
(SEE-yeh-loh)

These are her friends.
They play outside!
Fun!

Phrases to Know

Hello!
¡Hola!
(OH-lah)

Goodbye!
¡Adiós!
(ah-DEE-ohs)

Yes.
Sí.
(see)

No.
No.
(no)

Thank you!
¡Gracias!
(GRAH-see-ahs)

You're welcome.
De nada.
(deh NAH-dah)

My name is _____.
Me llamo _____.
(meh YAH-moh)

How are you?
¿Cómo estás?
(KOH-moh ehs-TAHS)

Colors

red **rojo** *(RROH-hoh)*	**orange** **naranja** *(nah-RAHN-hah)*	**yellow** **amarillo** *(ah-mah-REE-yoh)*	**green** **verde** *(VEHR-deh)*	**blue** **azul** *(ah-SOOL)*
purple **morado** *(moh-RAH-doh)*	**pink** **rosado** *(rroh-SAH-doh)*	**brown** **café** *(kah-FEH)*	**gray** **gris** *(grees)*	**black** **negro** *(NEH-groh)*

Numbers

1 **uno** *(OO-noh)*	**2** **dos** *(dohs)*	**3** **tres** *(trehs)*	**4** **cuatro** *(KWAH-troh)*	**5** **cinco** *(SEEN-koh)*
6 **seis** *(seys)*	**7** **siete** *(SEE-eh-teh)*	**8** **ocho** *(OH-choh)*	**9** **nueve** *(NWEH-veh)*	**10** **diez** *(DEE-ehs)*

Index

apple
manzana
(mahn-SAH-nah)

To Learn More

Finding more information is as easy as 1, 2, 3.

❶ Go to www.factsurfer.com

❷ Enter "myfirstlookatSpanish" into the search box.

❸ Click the "Surf" button to see a list of websites.